PARA ESPAÑOL
OPRIMA #2
SPEAKING SPANISH
IN TIMES OF
XENOPHOBIA

First published by Aussie Trading LLC
Copyright © 2024 by Juan Rodulfo
All rights reserved.
No part of this publication may be reproduced, stored, or transmitted in any form or by any means, electronic, mechanical, photocopying, recording, scanning or otherwise without written permission from the publisher. It is illegal to copy this book, publish it on a website, or distribute it by any other means without permission.
Juan Rodulfo has no responsibility for the persistence or accuracy of URLs of external or third-party Internet websites referenced in this publication and does not warrant that the content of such websites is, or will remain, accurate or appropriate.
The names used by companies to distinguish their products are often claimed as trademarks. All trademarks and product names used in this book and on its cover, trade names, service marks, trademarks are trademarks of their respective owners. The publishers and the book are not associated with any products or suppliers mentioned in this book. None of the companies or organizations referenced in the book have endorsed it.
Library of Congress Catalog
Names: Rodulfo, Juan
ISBN: 979-8-3483-8313-8 (paperback)
ISBN: 979-8-3483-8312-1 (e-book)
ISBN: 979-8-3483-8315-2 (hardcover)
First edition
Layout by Juan Rodulfo
Cover art by Guaripete Solutions
Production: Aussie Trading, LLC
books@aussietrading.ltd
Printed in the USA

juanrodulfo.com

Content

PREFACE 9
WE ARE ALL AFRICANS, LOL! 18
   Dispersal of modern Homo sapiens. 19
   Evidence 24
      Evidence from molecular biology. 24
      Genetics 26
      Evidence from the fossil record.... 27
      Inter-species breeding 30
   Science vs. Religion............................ 33
      What is science? 33
      What is religion? 33
      What is the difference between science and religion? 34
THE LANGUAGES ADVANTAGE 40
   Languages and Business................... 41
      English- The Language of Globalization... 42
      Mandarin- The Language that's Dying to Spend its Money 43
      Spanish- The Language of the Fastest Growing American Market Segment 44
      German- The Language of European Industrial Strength 45

Portuguese- A Continent of Opportunity 45
Arabic- The Web's Fastest-Growing Language 46
French- The Former English 47
Japanese 48
Russian- The Language of Trade and Diplomacy 48
Hindi... 49
Languages and Brain 50
To the left cortex and beyond 54
Change that's good for the brain ..55
The brain is plastic, it's fantastic .. 57

LEGAL ALIEN...63
Alien Categories 68
Common law jurisdictions........... 69
Other jurisdictions 72

SIZE MATTERS 77
US Population Statistics 78
White population decline..............78
A new "minority white" generation 79
Declines of white youth................ 80
U.S. Hispanic population............. 82

U.S. counties with largest Hispanic population, 2018 84

Latinos and Elections 86

Many more Latinos voted for Democrats than Republicans in 2018 U.S. 86

About a quarter of Hispanic voters cast a ballot in a midterm for the first time in 2018 86

Hispanic women more often voted for Democrats than Hispanic men in 2018 87

THE AMERICAN DREAM LANGUAGE 93

The Author 103

Publications: 104

Books: 104

Blogs: 104

Audiovisual Productions: 105

Podcasts: 105

Music: 105

Photography & Video: 105

Social Media Profiles: 105

References 107

juanrodulfo.com

PREFACE

As a Ride Share Driver, waiting for somebody to show on the App, I had plenty of time to meditate about important subjects that have been difficult to solve since the beginnings of Humanity, like for example: Who was first?, The Egg or the Hen?.

After years of discussion, research and study, I've came to the conclusion that nobody knows and nobody will, determine WHO IS IMMIGRANT OR NATIONAL, since the Evolution Theory comes with the cell growing and evolving from it through Earlier Apes (Nakalipithecus), Ouranophitecus (Gorilla Split) , Sahelanthropus (Possibly Bipedal), Orrorin (Chimpanzee Split), in the Hominini Stage Miocene Age, then the Homo Habilis Stage of the Pliocene Age including the Ardipithecus & Australophitecus (Earliest Bipedal and use of Stone Tools), and the Pleistocene Age starting with the Homo Erectus (Exit from Africa and Earliest fire use), following the Homo Heidelbergensis (Earliest Clothes and Cooking), the Neanderthals and the Homo sapiens which characterize as Modern Humans/Speech, as published in Wikipedia[i], some religions still believe that there is a God who created a Man, then took out his rib and made a Woman, in some place (With unknown coordinates) named Eden, then the Woman ate

juanrodulfo.com

an apple a snake gave her and they both were kicked out from that place and sent somewhere else, even if I believe this theory, who can answer me who is the IMMIGRANT, if they then began to populate our Planet with their descendants?

I'm actually living in Huntersville, NC, and working as an Entrepreneur, and depending on my finances go and drive to make some cash flow thanks to the Ride Share Economy, and I started no notice the frequency of the question: Where are you from?, which is like the frequent Question when you are some "Professional" or "Academic" environments: What are you? And the inquirer wished response must be: I am an Engineer, I am a Doctor, I am a Paper Hanging on my Office Wall, I am a Human you Moron don't you tell? But this is not his or her fault, is the way the Society raised our Parents, and their Parents raised them as a consequence of the Industrial Revolution, that sent a bunch of Humans to their homes for a lack of a "Diploma" or "Title", so they adopted the cruel sentence: "Study, so you will be "somebody" in life", pushing to the margin those who could not get a "Diploma" or "Title", or simple wanted to be any other thing than a student to satisfy their Parents/Families/Society Standards. The Question should be: Are you familiar with this job? Yes.

So the question "Where are you from" may have infinites reasons, curiosity, ice breaking to start a conversation, sympathy, you are a Human Behavior daily student like me or Racism...!, I used to answer: I'm from Venezuela, South America, and bla, bla, bla.

One of the first Jobs I was able to take as IMMIGRANT was Plotter Operator in a Decals Factory because I speak English and was supposed to understand the Instructions of the Lady in charge of the area and the use of those machines; I remember that one day she asked me: Are you American? And I answered: Yes, her face changed expressions from: You Immigrant to WTH? and remade the question: American? From where?, I with the Ironic Smurf sitting on my right shoulder said: Venezuela, and shot back again: Where is Venezuela?, this time with the Super Woman bracelet I repealed her bullet answering: South America, the room lights started tilting like in Stranger Things and the Lady became into Hugo Weaving the Agent Smith of Matrix and with his .50 shot: But I Pay Taxes!, and with the Neo Slow Motion Speed I falling on my back to avoid the bullets answered: I do pay taxes also, I'm paying them since I bought my first airplane ticket to the US, stood up and went back to my Plotter, the Agent Smith released her body and she came back to her Plotter.

Anybody in this country that takes money out of his pocket to buy even a water bottle is paying taxes; only the richest[ii] even making rivers of money cheat on the IRS.

I was born in Venezuela, visited Colombia and Ecuador and never experienced racism for being black, or aboriginal, or white, in fact my Mum Briceida, uses to call me "Negrito" which means something like little black, because she is "white", my Dad Eladio is "brown[iii]", so she had two "whites": Gustavo and Gabriela and two "blacks": Katiuska and me, being back there I heard from the KKK barely in a History Class or in the Movie: O Brother, Where Art Thou, (which I like so much is one of the few movies I can see again and again),

I was sure that was a thing of the XIX Century, but surprise, surprise! I came to the US and the KKK is like Dunkin Donuts, everywhere...

Thanks to Trevor Noah, John Oliver, Bill Maher, Lewis Black, Wyatt Cenac, Michael Moore, Noam Chomsky and others, from comedy to seriousness I've expanded my points of view of the world we live in, and especially enjoyed the Bill Maher chapter called Trump's Wall of Lies, that inspired me to gather the data and publish this book, where he goes like:

"The problem is Trump fans do not want a fence, or a river, or a virtual barrier, they want a fucking wall! Because a wall represents

an impregnable barrier that keeps out not just Mexicans but everything that makes them feel anxious about 'the old America that's slipping away.'

'The Wall, it is like one of those prescriptions drugs that blocks the causes of your discomfort. Yes, now there's Mexigone. Mexigone has been clinically proven to reduce the pain caused by foreigners entering the country illegally. Mexigone works with your natural gullibility to construct a wall that keeps immigrants from shithole countries out and good-paying jobs in so you can back clean your guns and sending out Facebook memes of Hillary getting hit with a golf ball.'

Except, it does not work that way. Most illegals do not even cross the border, they come here the same way you got back from Cabo. They catch a flight and then they just stay. Like that Australian on your couch.

Even Trump admitted The Wall was bogus when he was caught on tape to a call to Mexico's president saying the wall is the least important thing we are talking about. It was always just an applause line that got out of hand.

So, there you have it: The Wall will not help with employment, it is not feasible to build, and even Trump knows it is bullshit. And if all of that is not enough to deter you, let me add this Trumpsters, you do not need it, because everything that wall represents, the bigotry, the racism, the ignorance, the paranoia, is already in your heart.

Yes, The Wall has been inside you the whole time. Trump just brought it out because he is the jackass whisperer. But you do not need it. Every time you vote for a child molester because the other choice is a Democrat, The Wall is there. Every time you feel rage because a voice recording says, 'for Spanish press 2,' The Wall is there. It is there when you begin a Facebook post with, 'I'm not a racist, but.' And it is there every time a unisex bathroom makes you hold it until you get home. It's there when snow makes you deny global warming. And it is there at the ballgame when two gays on the kiss cam make you throw up in your mouth.

Every time you use air quotes when you say the word "college," The Wall is there. It is there when you use Jew as a verb. And it is there every time you are Tucker Carlson. So, you do not need a wall because, you see, even without it you are still the grumpy asshole who ruins Thanksgiving[iv].

This is not normal, not even must be a real thing, that's why, with the exception of this Ride Share Customer, Veteran Black Gentleman who served to the US Military deployed in Rwanda the years of the Genocide, wisely asked me: What do you call home?, that left me with no ironical answers, But! when somebody jumps into my car and asks: Where are you from? I answer: Planet Earth!

Figure 1. Bill Maher: The Wall Not Needed Because Bigotry, Racism, Ignorance & Paranoia Is in Heart of Every Trumpster

If you talk to a man in a language he understands, that goes to his head. If you talk to him in his language, that goes to his heart. **Nelson Mandela**

juanrodulfo.com

17

WE ARE ALL AFRICANS, LOL!

I knew I was family of Gorillas, and publicly claimed it on my book Manual for Gorillas: 9 Rules to be the "Fer-pect" Dictator, but now, on this research found that, based on the Evolution Theory we are all from AFRICAAAAAA!, Jajajajaja, I knew it!.

Wakanda Forever!

The study published on Wikipedia, titled: Human Evolution established that:

Anthropologists in the 1980s were divided regarding some details of reproductive barriers and migratory dispersals of the genus Homo. Subsequently, genetics has been used to investigate and resolve these issues. According to the Sahara pump theory evidence suggests that genus Homo have migrated out of Africa at least three and possibly four times (e.g., Homo erectus, Homo heidelbergensis and two or three times for Homo sapiens). Recent evidence suggests these dispersals are closely related to fluctuating periods of climate change.

Recent evidence suggests that humans may have left Africa half a million years earlier than previously thought. A joint Franco-Indian team has found human artifacts in the Siwalk Hills north of New Delhi dating back at least 2.6 million years. This is earlier than the previous earliest finding of genus Homo at Dmanisi, in Georgia, dating to 1.85 million years. Although controversial, tools found at a Chinese cave strengthen the case that humans used tools as far back as 2.48 million years ago. This suggests that the Asian "Chopper" tool tradition, found in Java and northern China may have left Africa before the appearance of the Acheulian hand axe.

DISPERSAL OF MODERN HOMO SAPIENS

Up until the genetic evidence became available there were two dominant models for the dispersal of modern humans. The multiregional hypothesis proposed that the genus Homo contained only a single interconnected population as it does today (not separate species), and that its evolution took place worldwide continuously over the last couple of million years. This model was proposed in 1988 by Milford H. Wolpoff. In contrast the "out of Africa" model proposed that modern H. sapiens habited in Africa recently (that is, approximately 200,000 years ago) and the subsequent migration through Eurasia resulted in nearly complete replacement of other Homo species. Chris B. Stringer and Peter Andrews developed this model.

Sequencing mtDNA and Y-DNA sampled from a wide range of Indigenous populations revealed ancestral information relating to both male and female genetic heritage and **strengthened the Out of Africa theory and weakened the views of Multiregional Evolutionism**. Aligned in genetic tree differences were interpreted as supportive of a recent single origin. Analyses have shown a greater diversity of DNA patterns throughout Africa, consistent with the idea that Africa is the ancestral home of mitochondrial Eve and Y-chromosomal Adam, and that modern human dispersal out of Africa has only occurred over the last 55,000 years.

"Out of Africa" has thus gained much support from research using female mitochondrial DNA and the male Y chromosome. After analyzing genealogy trees constructed using 133 types of mtDNA, researchers concluded that all were descended from a female African progenitor, dubbed Mitochondrial Eve. "Out of Africa" is also supported by the fact that mitochondrial genetic diversity is highest among African populations.

A broad study of African genetic diversity, headed by Sarah Tishkoff, found the San people had the greatest genetic diversity among the 113 distinct populations sampled, making them one of 14 "ancestral population clusters". The research also located a possible origin of modern human migration in south-western Africa, near the coastal border of Namibia and Angola. The fossil evidence was insufficient for archaeologist Richard Leakey to resolve the debate about exactly where in Africa modern humans first appeared. Studies of haplogroups in Y-chromosomal DNA and mitochondrial DNA have largely supported a recent African origin. All the evidence from autosomal DNA also predominantly supports a Recent African origin. However, evidence for archaic admixture in modern humans, both in Africa and later, throughout Eurasia has recently been suggested by a number of studies.

Recent sequencing of Neanderthal and Denisovan genomes shows that some admixture with these populations has occurred. Modern humans outside Africa have 2–4% Neanderthal alleles in their genome, and some Melanesians have an additional 4–6% of Denisovan alleles. These new results do not contradict the "out of Africa" model, except in its strictest interpretation, although they make the situation more complex. After recovery from a genetic bottleneck that some researchers speculate might be linked to the Toba super volcano catastrophe, a small group left Africa and interbred with Neanderthals, probably in the Middle East, on the Eurasian steppe or even in North Africa before their departure. Their still predominantly African descendants spread to populate the world. A fraction in turn interbred with Denisovans, probably in south-east Asia, before populating Melanesia. HLA haplotypes of Neanderthal and Denisova origin have been identified in modern Eurasian and Oceanian populations. The Denisovan EPAS1 gene has also been found in Tibetan populations. Studies of the human genome using machine learning have identified additional genetic contributions in Eurasians from an "unknown" ancestral population potentially related to the Neanderthal-Denisovan lineage.

There are still differing theories on whether there was a single exodus from Africa or several. A multiple dispersal model involves the Southern Dispersal theory, which has gained support in recent years from genetic, linguistic, and archaeological evidence. In this theory, there was a coastal dispersal of modern humans from the Horn of Africa crossing the Bab el Mandib to Yemen at a lower sea level around 70,000 years ago. This group helped to populate Southeast Asia and Oceania, explaining the discovery of early human sites in these areas much earlier than those in the Levant. This group seems to have been dependent upon marine resources for their survival.

Stephen Oppenheimer has proposed a second wave of humans may have later dispersed through the Persian Gulf oases, and the Zagros Mountains into the Middle East. Alternatively, it may have come across the Sinai Peninsula into Asia, from shortly after 50,000 yrs BP, resulting in the bulk of the human populations of Eurasia. It has been suggested that this second group possibly possessed a more sophisticated "big game hunting" tool technology and was less dependent on coastal food sources than the original group. Much of the evidence for the first group's expansion would have been destroyed by the rising sea levels at the end of each glacial maximum. The multiple dispersal model is contradicted by studies indicating that the populations of Eurasia and the populations of Southeast Asia and Oceania are all descended from the same mitochondrial DNA L3 lineages, which support a single migration out of Africa that gave rise to all non-African populations.

Stephen Oppenheimer, on the basis of the early date of Badoshan Iranian Aurignacian, suggests that this second dispersal, may have occurred with a pluvial period about 50,000 years before the present, with modern human big-game hunting cultures spreading up the Zagros Mountains, carrying modern human genomes from Oman, throughout the Persian Gulf, northward into Armenia and Anatolia, with a variant travelling south into Israel and to Cyrenicia.

EVIDENCE

The evidence on which scientific accounts of human evolution are based comes from many fields of natural science. The main source of knowledge about the evolutionary process has traditionally been the fossil record, but since the development of genetics beginning in the 1970s, DNA analysis has come to occupy a place of comparable importance. The studies of ontogeny, phylogeny and especially evolutionary developmental biology of both vertebrates and invertebrates offer considerable insight into the evolution of all life, including how humans evolved. The specific study of the origin and life of humans is anthropology, particularly paleoanthropology which focuses on the study of human prehistory.

EVIDENCE FROM MOLECULAR BIOLOGY

Family tree showing the extant hominoids: humans (genus Homo), chimpanzees and bonobos (genus Pan), gorillas (genus Gorilla), orangutans (genus Pongo), and gibbons (four genera of the family Hylobatidae: Hylobates, Hoolock, Nomascus, and Symphalangus). All except gibbons are hominids.

The closest living relatives of humans are bonobos and chimpanzees (both genus Pan) and gorillas (genus Gorilla). With the sequencing of both the human and chimpanzee genome, as of 2012 estimates of the similarity between their DNA sequences range between 95% and 99%. By using the technique called the molecular clock which estimates the time required for the number of divergent mutations to accumulate between two lineages, the approximate date for the split between lineages can be calculated.

The gibbons (family Hylobatidae) and then orangutans (genus Pongo) were the first groups to split from the line leading to the hominins, including humans—followed by gorillas, and, ultimately, by the chimpanzees (genus Pan). The splitting date between hominin and chimpanzee lineages is placed by some between 4 to 8 million years ago, that is, during the Late Miocene. Speciation, however, appears to have been unusually drawn-out. Initial divergence occurred sometime between 7 to 13 million years ago, but ongoing hybridization blurred the separation and delayed complete separation during several millions of years. Patterson (2006) dated the final divergence at 5 to 6 million years ago.

Genetic evidence has also been employed to resolve the question of whether there was any gene flow between early modern humans and Neanderthals, and to enhance our understanding of the early human migration patterns and splitting dates. By comparing the parts of the genome that are not under natural selection, and which therefore accumulate mutations at a steady rate, it is possible to reconstruct a genetic tree incorporating the entire human species since the last shared ancestor.

Each time a certain mutation (single-nucleotide polymorphism) appears in an individual and is passed on to his or her descendants a haplogroup is formed including all the descendants of the individual who will also carry that mutation. By comparing mitochondrial DNA, which is inherited only from the mother, geneticists have concluded that the last female common ancestor whose genetic marker is found in all modern humans, the so-called mitochondrial Eve, must have lived around 200,000 years ago.

GENETICS

Main articles: Human evolutionary genetics and Human genetic variation

Human evolutionary genetics studies how one human genome differs from the other, the evolutionary past that gave rise to it, and its current effects. Differences between genomes have anthropological, medical, and forensic implications and applications. Genetic data can provide important insight into human evolution.

EVIDENCE FROM THE FOSSIL RECORD

There is little fossil evidence for the divergence of the gorilla, chimpanzee, and hominin lineages. The earliest fossils that have been proposed as members of the hominin lineage are Sahelanthropus tchadensis dating from seven million years ago, Orrorin tugenensis dating from 5.7 million years ago, and Ardipithecus kadabba dating to 5.6 million years ago. Each of these have been argued to be a bipedal ancestor of later hominins but, in each case, the claims have been contested. It is also possible that one or more of these species are ancestors of another branch of African apes, or that they represent a shared ancestor between hominins and other apes.

The question then of the relationship between these early fossil species and the hominin lineage is still to be resolved. From these early species, the australopithecines arose around four million years ago and diverged into robust (also called Paranthropus) and gracile branches, one of which (possibly A. garhi) probably went on to become ancestors of the genus Homo. The australopithecine species that is best represented in the fossil record is Australopithecus afarensis with more than one hundred fossil individuals represented, found from Northern Ethiopia (such as the famous "Lucy"), to Kenya, and South Africa. Fossils of robust australopithecines such as Au. robustus (or alternatively Paranthropus robustus) and Au./P. boisei are particularly abundant in South Africa at sites such as Kromdraai and Swartkrans, and around Lake Turkana in Kenya.

The earliest member of the genus Homo is Homo habilis which evolved around 2.8 million years ago. Homo habilis is the first species for which we have positive evidence of the use of stone tools. They developed the Oldowan lithic technology, named after the Olduvai Gorge in which the first specimens were found. Some scientists consider Homo rudolfensis[v], a larger bodied group of fossils with similar morphology to the original H. habilis fossils, to be a separate species while others consider them to be part of H. habilis—simply representing intraspecies variation, or perhaps even sexual dimorphism. The brains of these early hominins were about the same size as that of a chimpanzee, and their main adaptation was bipedalism as an adaptation to terrestrial living.

During the next million years, a process of encephalization began and, by the arrival (about 1.9 million years ago) of Homo erectus in the fossil record, cranial capacity had doubled. Homo erectus were the first of the hominins to emigrate from Africa, and, from 1.8 to 1.3 million years ago, this species spread through Africa, Asia, and Europe. One population of H.

erectus, also sometimes classified as a separate species Homo ergaster, remained in Africa and evolved into Homo sapiens. It is believed that these species, H. erectus and H. ergaster, were the first to use fire and complex tools.

The earliest transitional fossils between H. ergaster/erectus and archaic H. sapiens are from Africa, such as Homo rhodesiensis, but seemingly transitional forms were also found at Dmanisi, Georgia. These descendants of African H. erectus spread through Eurasia from ca. 500,000 years ago evolving into H. antecessor, H. heidelbergensis and H. neanderthalensis. The earliest fossils of anatomically modern humans are from the Middle Paleolithic, about 200,000 years ago such as the Omo remains of Ethiopia; later fossils from Es Skhul cave in Israel and Southern Europe begin around 90,000 years ago (0.09 million years ago).

As modern humans spread out from Africa, they encountered other hominins such as Homo neanderthalensis and the so-called Denisovans, who may have evolved from populations of Homo erectus that had left Africa around two million years ago. The nature of interaction between early humans and these sister species has been a long-standing source of controversy, the question being whether humans replaced these earlier species or whether they were in fact similar enough to interbreed, in which case these earlier populations may have contributed genetic material to modern humans.

This migration out of Africa is estimated to have begun about 70,000 years BP and modern humans subsequently spread globally, replacing earlier hominins either through competition or hybridization. They inhabited Eurasia and Oceania by 40,000 years BP, and the Americas by at least 14,500 years BP.

INTER-SPECIES BREEDING

Further information: Interbreeding between archaic and modern humans.

The hypothesis of interbreeding, also known as hybridization, admixture, or hybrid-origin theory, has been discussed ever since the discovery of Neanderthal remains in the 19th century. The linear view of human evolution began to be abandoned in the 1970s as different species of humans were discovered that made the linear concept increasingly unlikely. In the 21st century with the advent of molecular biology techniques and computerization, whole-genome sequencing of Neanderthal and human genome was performed, confirming recent admixture between different human species. In 2010, evidence based on molecular biology was published, revealing unambiguous examples of interbreeding between archaic and modern humans during the Middle Paleolithic and early Upper Paleolithic. It has been demonstrated that interbreeding happened in several independent events that included Neanderthals and Denisovans, as well as several unidentified hominins. Today, approximately 2% of DNA from most Europeans and Asians is Neanderthal, with traces of Denisovan heritage. Also, 4–6% of modern Melanesian genetics are Denisovan. Comparisons of the human genome to the genomes of Neanderthals, Denisovans and apes can help identify features that set modern humans apart from other hominin species. In a 2016 comparative genomics study, a Harvard Medical School/UCLA research team made a world map on the distribution and made some predictions about where Denisovan and Neanderthal genes may be impacting modern human biology.

    For example, comparative studies in the mid-2010s found several traits related to neurological, immunological, developmental, and metabolic phenotypes that were developed by archaic humans to European and Asian environments and inherited to modern humans through admixture with local hominins.

    Although the narratives of human evolution are often contentious, several discoveries since 2010 show that human evolution should not be seen as a simple linear or branched progression, but a mix of related species. In fact, genomic research has shown that hybridization between substantially diverged lineages is the rule, not the exception, in human evolution. Furthermore, it is argued that hybridization was an essential creative force in the emergence of modern humans.[vi]

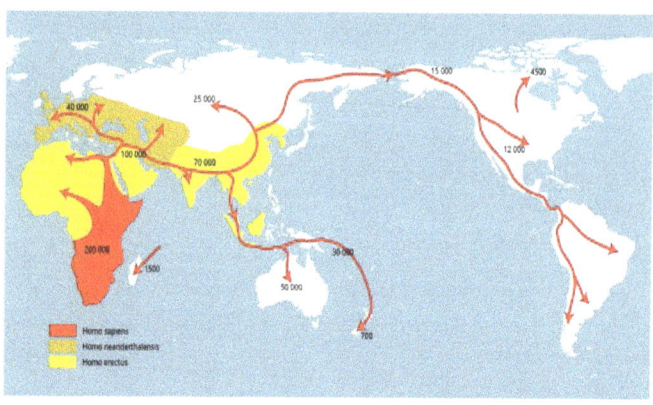

Figure 2. Here we clearly see frontiers, borders, and ICE Control Points of Homo Sapiens Migrations since 200K Years ago.

This is the African-Center-Evolution explanation, we should have begun from differentiating Science from Religion, to be fair with both audiences.

The Smithsonian National Museum of Natural History, published an article about Science, Religion, Evolution and Creationism, dated from 2018, where Drs. Connie Bertka & Jim Miller explained:

SCIENCE VS. RELIGION

WHAT IS SCIENCE?

Science is a way to understand nature by developing explanations for the structures, processes and history of nature that can be tested by observations in laboratories or in the field. Sometimes such observations are direct, like measuring the chemical composition of a rock. Other times these observations are indirect, like determining the presence of an exoplanet through the wobble of its host star. An explanation of some aspects of nature that have been well supported by such observations is a theory. Well-substantiated theories are the foundations of human understanding of nature. The pursuit of such understanding is science.

WHAT IS RELIGION?

Religion, or more appropriately religions, are cultural phenomena comprised of social institutions, traditions of practice, literatures, sacred texts and stories, and sacred places that identify and convey an understanding of ultimate meaning. Religions are very diverse. While it is common for religions to identify the ultimate with a deity (like the western monotheisms – Judaism, Christianity, Islam) or deities, not all do. There are non-theistic religions, like Buddhism.

WHAT IS THE DIFFERENCE BETWEEN SCIENCE AND RELIGION?

Although science does not provide proof, it does provide explanations. Science depends on deliberate, explicit, and formal testing (in the natural world) of explanations for the way the world is, for the processes that led to its present state, and for its possible future. When scientists see that a proposed explanation has been well confirmed by repeated observations, it serves the scientific community as a reliable theory. A theory in science is the highest form of scientific explanation, not just a "mere opinion." Strong theories, ones that have been well confirmed by evidence from nature, are an essential goal of science. Well-supported theories guide future efforts to solve other questions about the natural world.

Religions may draw upon scientific explanations of the world, in part, as a reliable way of knowing what the world is like, about which they seek to discern its ultimate meaning. However, "testing" of religious understandings of the world is incidental, implicit, and informal in the course of the life of the religious community in the world. Religious understanding draws from both subjective insight and traditional authority. Therefore, some people view religion as based on nothing more than opinion or "blind faith," and so, as immune to rational thought. However, this is an erroneous judgment. Virtually all the historic religions include traditions of rational reflection.

On their job, Drs. Connie Bertka & Jim Miller, give some hints about the concepts: Evolutionists and Creationists, separating both, and linking each one with Science and Religion respectively, determining that in principle all members of the three western monotheisms (Judaism, Christianity and Islam) are "creationists" in that they believe the order of nature exists because a reality beyond nature, commonly called "God", is the ultimate cause of all existence. In this sense of the word, many creationists accept an evolutionary understanding of natural history. However, at least four types of creationism can be identified, and each has a distinctive view of the evolutionary sciences and human origins.

"Young-Earth" creationists hold that the sacred text provides an inerrant account of how the universe, all life and humankind came into existence; namely, in six 24-hour days, some 6-10,000 years ago. Human beings were created through a direct act of divine intervention in the order of nature.

"Old-Earth" creationists hold that the sacred text is an infallible account of why the universe, all life and humankind came into existence, but accepts that the "days" of creation are metaphorical and could represent very long periods of time. While many aspects of nature may be the consequence of direct acts of divine creation, at very least they hold that the very beginning of the universe, the origin of life and the origin of humankind are the consequence of distinct acts of divine intervention in the order of nature.

Theistic evolutionists also hold that the sacred text provides an infallible account of why the universe, all life and humankind came into existence. However, they also hold that for the most part, the diversity of nature from stars to planets to living organisms, including the human body, is a consequence of the divine using processes of evolution to create indirectly. Still, for many who hold this position, the very beginning of the universe, the origin of life, and the origin of what is distinctive about humankind are the consequence of direct acts of divine intervention in the order of nature.

Evolutionary theists hold that the sacred text, while giving witness to the ultimate divine source of all of nature, in no way specifies the means of creation. Further, they hold that the witness of creation itself is that the divine creates only indirectly through evolutionary processes without any intervention in the order of nature[vii].

As we can see by ourselves, when you check the beginning of this, there were no borders, ICEs, Check Points, Passports,

Customs, Governments, Currencies, Colors, Races, just: Planet-Human-Nature...

The limits of my language mean the limits of my world.
Ludwig Wittgenstein

THE LANGUAGES ADVANTAGE

One of the foreigner customers[viii] I had as Ride Share Driver, told me that his father once tough him that the more languages he would learn, the more business he was going to be able to make.

With the Chinese Economy getting stronger and stronger, with the Indians dominating the tech scenario, and the Latino Population increasing its size around the globe, it is IMPERATIVE for English Speakers to learn Spanish-Chinese-Hindi, even though my son was arguing with me about the importance of German as a Biz-Tech Language.

LANGUAGES AND BUSINESS

In an article published by Startupr Hong Kong Limited, on October 4, 2018, in Medium.com, titled: 10 Most Important Business Languages in Global Market[ix], the author establishes:

As the face of international business changes, so do the languages used to communicate. From professional networking and academic collaboration to transportation and traveling, the business world requires business owners to use different languages to scale up their companies. Even if you are a small company and aspiring to sell your services and products to different linguistic backgrounds and cultures, you need to take its content to the next multilingual level.

There are more than 6,000 languages worldwide, and it seems difficult to pick the most critical languages to impact your overall earnings. When you think about the languages you would like to learn for your business, your first assessment should be looking at your macro level business goals, core target audiences and thinking about how you see yourself in the coming years.

Your approach also needs to consider global connectivity and how you manage your global content as you devise a globalization strategy. As a matter of fact, languages such as Russian, French, English, Mandarin, and German have dominated the global landscape for doing business.

But these might not be the only important languages in the future. It is imperative to understand which languages are the most important and useful, which will open pathways for securing the most significant return on investments, and which ones will lead the way in the next 50 years.

If you need help deciding the most important languages for your business, we have compiled a handy list of the top ten languages that will help you in initiating global growth for business and marketing content translation.

ENGLISH- THE LANGUAGE OF GLOBALIZATION

English is the most influential language of academia and the business world, occupying the top in the field of languages and spoken by over three-quarters of the world's population. It is used in ninety-four countries by 339 million native speakers, and it is the de facto language of the United States and an official language of Australia, the United Kingdom, South Africa, and several other countries, making it an essential language for business owners.

Along with this, the English language also retains the number one spot as the most used language by 53% of websites and internet users with 949 million users. Hence, there is no denying the fact that English is the language of globalization, and crucial for those entrepreneurs who want to thrive on the global stage.

MANDARIN- THE LANGUAGE THAT'S DYING TO SPEND ITS MONEY

The Chinese language is the new boss in town, with the most significant number of native speakers (approximately 983 million speakers), while more than 1.2 billion people understand the Chinese Mandarin dialect. It is the one that you just cannot miss while talking about the best languages for business, as it is the second most popular language among internet users. If Asian markets continue to expand their internet usage, Chinese could be expected to supplant English as the most widely used internet language soon.

The rationale behind this trend is mainly due to the enormous economic shift that China has gone through in the past three decades, from national trade to international trade ties and cross-border treaties to huge leaps in the field of science and technology. And if this trend continues, analysts predict that China will become the world's leading economy by 2050.

SPANISH- THE LANGUAGE OF THE FASTEST GROWING AMERICAN MARKET SEGMENT

Believe it or not, the United States has recently been cited as the second largest Spanish-speaking country in the world, where an estimated 37.6 million people speak it as their first language. There is no denying that English is the primary language that comes to mind for the USA, but its fifty million Spanish speakers and their small and large businesses might remind you that it is not the only language spoken in the country.

As the US has the world's largest economy and the Hispanic population in the US is projected to double by 2050, this makes Spanish enormously important. If you are willing to start your business in the US, or indeed anywhere in the Western hemisphere, Spanish needs to be one of your chosen languages.

GERMAN- THE LANGUAGE OF EUROPEAN INDUSTRIAL STRENGTH

With the advancement of technology and networking opportunities, the German economy proves to be one of the strongest and stable within the European Union, with a GDP of over 2.4 trillion Euros. In fact, being able to speak German provides a significant advantage to anyone wanting to pursue international business. The German language is the fourth most used language by nearly ninety-five million native speakers and a total of 210 million speakers worldwide.

Not only is Germany one of the most populated countries within Europe, but there are also a large number of German-speaking people within the nearby nations of Belgium, Austria, Holland, Denmark, Switzerland, Liechtenstein, and Luxembourg. It is also estimated that the ability to speak German could come with a wage increase of about 4%.

PORTUGUESE- A CONTINENT OF OPPORTUNITY

Portuguese is one of the top ten most spoken languages in the world and the second most spoken language in Latin America behind Spanish. Portuguese is spoken around 215 million people in Portugal, Brazil, and some parts of Africa. As per the statistics, the Portuguese blasted forward with 6% share growth after several flat years and managed to come in fifth, with a whopping 154.5 million speakers.

For professional business owners, Brazil is the main attraction for doing business. Being the most widely cited science base outside the G8, Brazil has many opportunities to capitalize on scientific cooperation and collaboration, including in the areas of pharmaceuticals and energy.

It is the largest economy in Latin America, and there are some indicators that recovery is on its way in the next year or so, which means business opportunities there will only continue to grow. Portuguese is also gaining popularity in Asia due to the region's great diplomatic and economic relations with Portugal and the Lusophone countries. So, if you are aspiring to increase your sales and expand your business globally, learning the Portuguese language will be your best choice.

ARABIC- THE WEB'S FASTEST-GROWING LANGUAGE

As the official language of many Middle Eastern countries where business opportunities are growing fast, learning Arabic can be a big plus for business owners. 295 million speakers speak the Arabic language worldwide, and it is the official language of 28 different countries, including many dynamic, growing economies in the Middle East and Africa. In fact, in the UK's top fifty export market in goods, six Arabic speaking countries appear with a combined value to the economy that surpasses that of China, Italy and Spain. This is why in a report from the British Council, Arabic ranks as the second most important 'language of the future.'

FRENCH- THE FORMER ENGLISH

French is the official language of over twenty-nine countries throughout the world, and it is the second-most widely spoken first language in the European Union. The colonial history of France has helped spread this language throughout the modern world in the same way as English. This has led to a situation in which there are more non-native French speakers than native speakers.

The French-speaking world also includes Africa, which is proliferating and rich in natural resources. The top five fastest-growing African economies include Tanzania, Rwanda, Mozambique, the Democratic Republic of Congo, and Cote D'Ivoire, which French is an official language in three of them. While it is not as prevalent globally as it once was, there is no question that France will remain one of the United Kingdom's most important trade partners. French language skills are both necessary and essential for businesses here, and it remains one of the top languages to learn.

JAPANESE

Another Asian language with a bright prospect is Japanese with 130 million native speakers and an equal number of non-native speakers spread out in the world. It is also the sixth language for internet users with e-commerce sales of $88.06 billion. Being the world's second largest investor in research and development, Japan is one of the most technologically advanced and integrated nations in the world.

In fact, Japan is renowned as a significant contributor to UK prosperity, both as a substantial investor and an export marketer by the British Council. Although the economy of Japan has revealed some signs of stagnation, it is pertinent not to dismay the ingenuity of Japanese businesses, where, like Germany, Japan has a reputation for excellence in the science and technology sectors. Japan remains at the forefront of cutting-edge electronics scene and robotics, and speaking Japanese is ideal for many opportunities in these fields.

RUSSIAN- THE LANGUAGE OF TRADE AND DIPLOMACY

With 160 million native speakers throughout central and Eastern Europe and in Russia, it is the ninth most common language in the world and the second most used in website content after English. Due to the historical power of the Soviet Union, Russian is an official language of the United Nations and cited as the most influential Slavonic language in history. The Russian language is also widely used in many of the post-Soviet states, which provides access to new and up-in-coming business potential.

Russian's importance is not only due to its large number of native speakers but also to the undeniable political and economic power of Russia. With a deep oil and gas reserves and rich culture, and enormous potential for real estate investment, Russian is one of the best languages to learn for anyone who wants to grow their business into one of the most powerful countries on Earth.

Hindi

Finally, Hindi is the tenth most-spoken language in the world, with 270 million native speakers. But you must be curious why would Hindi be one of the top languages for your localization strategy and business translation? Although India is home to 126 million English speakers, around 85% of the population does not speak English well, and it has been outpaced using local languages. According to CSA Research report, Hindi increased a massive 67% on the latest on the Top of one hundred online languages, mostly due to investment by the government, mobile web penetration, and other initiatives on the subcontinent. All this has set the pace for Hindi on the global stage.

LANGUAGES AND BRAIN

The non-English immigrant that comes into the US, needs to learn and make business in English, so now has two languages, increasing his competitive advantage against those who only speak one language.

Bec Crew published an article in 2014[x], about the results of a study conducted by Penn State University's Researchers stating that learning a language will change the structure of the brain, making it more efficient and these improvements can be experienced at any age.

Every time you learn something new, you strengthen your brain. Just like physical exercise strengthens your various muscles, tissues, and organs, the more you exercise specific areas in the brain, the stronger and more connected those areas will become.

The Penn State team decided to observe the brain activity of native English-speakers as they went through the process of learning Chinese - specifically, Mandarin - vocabulary. They gathered thirty-nine volunteers of varying ages and scanned their brains over a six-week period as half of them took part in language lessons and the other half acted as control subjects. The participants were put through two functional magnetic resonance imaging (fMRI) scans, one before the experiment began and then another one after six weeks, and the team observed the physical changes that had occurred.

The team found that, compared to the group that did not participate in the language lessons, the group that did had undergone several structural and functional changes in their brains. First off, their brain networks have become better integrated, which means they are more flexible and allow for faster and more efficient learning. They also found that those who excelled in the language lessons had more integrated networks than the brains of those who struggled, even before the experiment had begun, suggesting that they habitually sought out new things to learn and exercise their brains with.

The way the researchers determined the level of connectivity and efficiency of their participants' brain networks was by analyzing the strength and direction of the connections between specific regions of the brain that become active in learning. The stronger these connections - or edges - are between one area to the next, the faster and more efficiently they can work together as a whole network.

The team also found that the language-learning participants ended up with increased density in their grey matter and that their white matter tissue had been strengthened. Grey matter is a type of neural tissue that encompasses various regions in the brain associated with muscle control, memory formation, emotions, and sensory perception such as seeing and hearing, and it's white matter's job to connect these grey matter regions together in the brain's cerebrum, sort of like a train line for your brain.

"The evidence reviewed so far portrays a picture that is highly consistent with structural neuroplasticity observed for other domains," the team concludes in the Journal of Neurolinguistics. "Second language experience-induced brain changes, including increased grey matter (GM) density and white matter (WM) integrity, can be found in children, young adults, and the elderly; can occur rapidly with short-term language learning or training; and are sensitive to age, age of acquisition, proficiency or performance level, language-specific characteristics, and individual differences."

The researchers are now working on figuring out how to teach language in new, very different ways to maximize these functional and structural changes in the brain, including the use of 3D virtual environments.

"A very interesting finding is that, contrary to previous studies, the brain is much more plastic than we thought," said lead researcher and professor of psychology, linguistics and information sciences and technology, Ping Li, in a press release. "We can still see anatomical changes in the brain (in the elderly), which is very encouraging news for ageing."

Raquel Magalhães, in her article: "What happens to your brain when you learn a new language?"[xi], notes that learning a second language makes us smarter.

In 2013, a group of researchers from the University of Edinburgh published the largest study to date about the correlation between bilingualism and progression of dementia and other cognitive diseases like Alzheimer's. The subjects were 648 patients from Hyderabad, the capital city of the state of Telangana, in India. Telugu and Urdu are the predominant languages in that region, where English is also commonly used. Most of the residents of Hyderabad are bilingual, 391 of whom were part of the study. The conclusion was that the bilingual patients had developed dementia, on average, four and a half years later than the monolingual ones, strongly suggesting that bilingualism has a deep impact on neurological structures and processes.

The process of acquiring a second language might be one we dedicate a lot of time and effort to, at school for example, but in some cases, it happens naturally (picking up French after moving to Paris, for instance). So how can it be that this process, regardless of how it takes place, has such a big impact on the brain?

TO THE LEFT CORTEX AND BEYOND

It has long been established that humans' capacity to use their native language is stored in the left hemisphere of the brain in over 90% of the normal population. The main parts of the brain involved in language processes are the Broca's area, located in the left frontal lobe, which is responsible for speech production and articulation, and the Wernicke's area, in the left temporal lobe, associated with language development and comprehension.

Language learning, however, is a complex procedure that scientists have determined is not limited to any hemisphere of the brain, but instead involves information exchange between the left and right sides. Nothing comes as a surprise if we consider just how many elements a single language entail.

The professor of Psychology and Linguistics at Pennsylvania State University Dr. Ping Li explains that full knowledge of a language includes remembering the words (lexicon), learning its sound system (phonology), acquiring the writing system (orthography), getting familiar with the grammar (syntax) and picking up the subtle ways to express oneself (pragmatics). These distinct linguistic elements require the brain to activate different parts, including the frontal and parietal cortical regions, the frontal and temporal regions, the occipital and temporal-parietal regions and the frontal and subcortical regions. Also involved in the process is the corpus callosum, a white matter pathway that connects the left and the right hemispheres, enabling the transfer and integration of information between them.

But the complexity does not stop here. The part of the brain where humans store a second language varies according to the age, they acquire it. A study conducted at the Memorial Sloan-Kettering Cancer Center in New York with the help of twelve bilingual volunteers revealed that children who learn a second language early on store it together with their native language, while in adult learners it is saved in a different area of the brain. This suggests that the brain accommodates languages separately at different points of the subject's lifespan, which means the structures involved in language acquisition and processing are not fixed, but change, undergoing cortical adaptation when a new language is added.

CHANGE THAT'S GOOD FOR THE BRAIN

The process of learning something influences the brain like the one exercising has on the muscles. If we make them move, they increase in size and become stronger. The same thing happens to the brain. By putting it to work, we are making it alter its structure, while at the same time improving certain functions. Because language learning is such a complex process, the brain regions involved in it are enhanced. This is reflected in an increase of white and gray matter (that contains most of the brain's neurons and synapses) in said regions.

When it comes to the corpus callosum, for instance, several studies suggest that the data transfer between the left and the right hemispheres that happens during the acquisition of a second language contributes to an increase in its white matter volume and in the number of fibers that provide greater cortical connectivity.

For people who speak more than one language, it takes imperceptible effort to switch between them. This mental exercise appears to be what boosts gray matter volume in other regions of the brain. Further research conducted by Dr. Ping Li shows that the anterior cingulate cortex increases in size because of the important role it plays in monitoring which language is being spoken and keeping the other language(s) from intruding on our speech.

Research on this topic has also been conducted at the Center for the Study of Learning at Georgetown University Medical Center. Lead by senior author Guinevere Eden, a team compared gray matter volume between adult bilinguals and monolinguals and was able to observe greater gray matter in the bilingual individuals' brains, specifically in frontal and parietal brain regions that are involved in executive control. Changes have further been observed in the dorsolateral prefrontal cortex of bilingual individuals. This is the region of the brain that plays a role in "executive function, problem solving, switching between tasks and focusing while filtering out irrelevant information," as explained by Mia Nacamulli in a Ted-Ed talk about the benefits of bilingualism.

THE BRAIN IS PLASTIC, IT'S FANTASTIC

For a very long time, scientists didn't believe it was possible for the brain to change throughout life. The overall assumption was that the brain would develop up until a certain point, from which its connections would become fixed and then eventually start to fade. It was also believed that there was no way to repair the brain after it suffered injury. However, recent studies proved the exact opposite: that the brain, in fact, never stops changing as a response to different experiences.

This is explained by the concept of neuroplasticity. In neuroscience, "plastic" refers to the capacity that materials must change and be molded into different shapes. It is the brain's ability to adjust its physical structure and, this way, repair damaged regions, grow new neurons, rezone regions to perform new tasks and build networks of neurons that allow us to remember, feel and dream things. It is, furthermore, what allows us to explain how the brain can mold itself following second language acquisition.

Neuroplasticity generally decreases as we grow older, which is why it is easier for children to become fluent in a second language than adults. The infant brain is more plastic, making it more easily adaptable and able to deal with the challenges of speaking two languages, like having to switch between one and the other in different contexts. This does not mean that adults should give up learning a new language all together, on the contrary. The benefits associated with brain changes due to learning have been observed in sequential bilinguals (people who learn their second language later in life) as well.

The changes to the brain are not felt like other changes in the body, such as growing pains, but translate into cognitive advantages. Learning a second language is, as mentioned before, a complex process that involves different brain regions and puts them to work. On top of that, once other languages are mastered, switching back and forth between them is more demanding on the brain. This mental gymnastics of sorts provides the brain with better compensatory mechanisms. The executive control center of the brain is what manages this dual or multiple language system, so as we learn how to use the right language at the right time, we are exercising the regions of the brain responsible for our executive function through neuroplasticity.

A stronger executive function means bilingual or multilingual individuals are generally better at analyzing their surroundings, multitasking, and problem solving. There's also evidence of them having a larger working memory even if the task at hand is not related to language. The biggest benefit, however, is the increased ability to cope with degenerative diseases like dementia or Alzheimer's, as demonstrated in several studies like the one mentioned in the beginning. This does not mean that the brains of bilinguals are not susceptible to cognitive degeneration, but they are better able to cope with the damage, thanks to the compensatory mechanisms arising from knowing, and using, a second language.

Oh, I'm an alien, I'm a legal alien.
I'm an Englishman in New York
Oh, I'm an alien, I'm a legal alien.
I'm an Englishman in New York.
Sting

LEGAL ALIEN

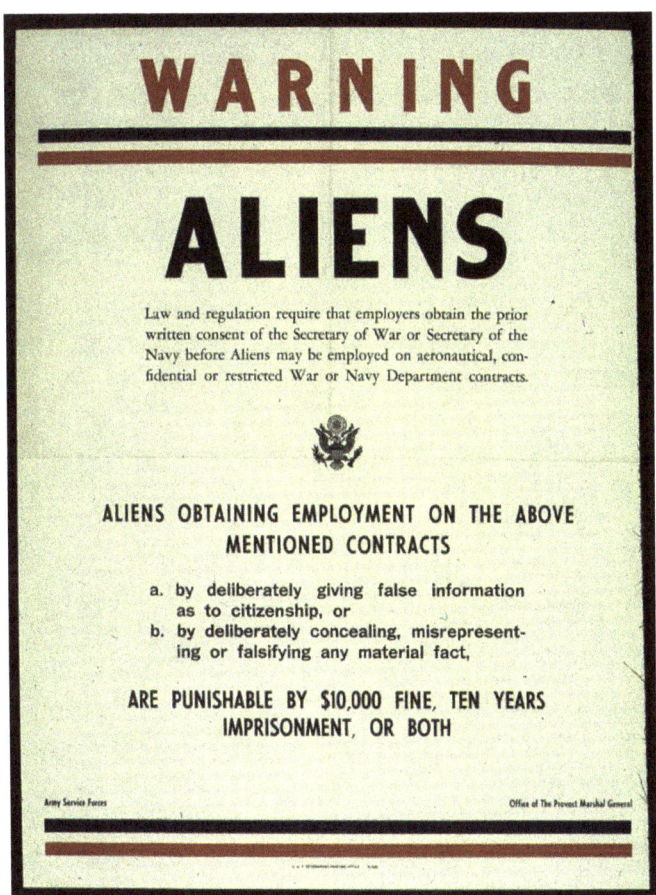

Figure 3.- World War II poster from the US.

The Immigration and Naturalization Service (INS) began issuing aliens an Alien Registration number in 1940, and on April 1, 1944, began using this number to create individual case files, called Alien Files or A-Files.

A-Files contain all records of any active case of an alien not yet naturalized as they passed through the United States immigration and inspection process. An A-File might also be created without any action taken by the alien; for example, if the INS initiated a law enforcement action against or involving the alien.[xii]

In her article: "This new year, let us stop using the word 'alien'", published on The Hill online by Elizabeth Rosenman[xiii], she expressed the following:

The first time I heard someone called an "alien" in a legal context was over breakfast with a roommate in law school. After college, she had spent a year playing basketball in France. Why leave such a cool job, I wondered. She explained that French law prohibits "alien" athletes from staying indefinitely.

The word "alien" sounded funny — it was not yet part of popular discourse in America in 1985, or not as a politically charged term for immigrants. When I seemed confused, she wiggled her index fingers above her ears, pretending to be an extraterrestrial.

It turned out that "alien" already existed in the law as a technical term for a noncitizen, but most people associated it instead with science fiction.

Although "alien" terminology has seeped into earlier immigration debates here, President Trump revitalized it in the 2016 election cycle by brandishing "alien" and "illegal aliens" to pit his supporters against asylum seekers and other immigrants.

Then, before the midterm elections, those words gained extra political heft because Republicans who uttered them were signaling, they backed the president's entire agenda, not just his hard-liner approach to immigration.

The word "alien" was codified in 1790, when President George Washington approved granting limited citizenship to an "alien" who is a "free white person" in our original Naturalization Act. The term stuck and is still used in the Act's current version and in various other statutes.

Our founding fathers borrowed "alien" from English jurist William Blackstone, who, in 1765, wrote that the English population was divided into "natural-born subjects...and aliens, such as are born out of it." For Washington, "alien" did not have any negative overtones.

Here is the problem. In recent years, the word has developed offensive and dehumanizing connotations. This is not the first time that our legal language has lagged in popular usage. Indeed, "Negro" and "Oriental" remained in federal law until 2016. But of course, those words were not being spoken in court or in mainstream media.

According to the Oxford English Dictionary, a human "alien" is "a foreigner, a stranger, an outsider" or someone who is "opposed, repugnant."

Although most news outlets no longer use "alien" to describe non-citizens, the word remains prominent in the far-right media. Breitbart and Fox News frequently call immigrants "illegal aliens" because they prefer language that encourages fear and distrust of immigrants.

At the Supreme Court, conservative Justices still freely use the term to refer to non-citizens. Recently, in a case about the detention of immigrants during deportation proceedings, Justice Samuel A. Alito Jr. said, "I can see the equities when the alien has been free for a number of years. But Congress, wisely or not, thought that this class of aliens was dangerous, and they should not be trusted."

The Department of Homeland Security also condones the word. In fact, it assigns non-citizens an Alien Registration Number (A-Number), which is a string of numbers preceded by the letter "A." A-Numbers have been used in this country since 1940, when Congress passed the Alien Registration Act. It became law during a time, like the present, when our government was particularly unwelcoming to people fleeing persecution.

In 1939, for instance, U.S. officials turned away a boat carrying 937 passengers, almost all Jewish refugees fleeing the Third Reich. More than a quarter of them eventually perished in the Holocaust. As anti-Semitism worsened in Europe, countless Jews sought refuge here. Many were rejected for allegedly posing a threat to national security.

At about the same time that the U.S. began using A-Numbers, the Nazis were tattooing a series of numbers, also preceded by the letter "A," onto the forearms of Hungarian Jews imprisoned at Auschwitz. For me, this chilling coincidence is reason enough to change the way we keep track of asylum seekers and other immigrants.

There's evidence that "alien" terminology is on its way out. In 2015, California expunged "alien" from its labor code. The following year, a group of Dartmouth college students convinced the Library of Congress to remove "alien" and "illegal alien" from its subject headings. But before less prejudicial terms could be added, Republicans from the House Appropriations Committee demanded that the library reverse course.

In January, when Democrats have the majority in the House of Representatives, it is the right time to reinstate the Library of Congress's decision to strike "alien." And with all the baggage the term carries, we should urge friends and colleagues to make a New Year's Resolution to ditch it in favor of words like "noncitizen" or "asylum seeker" or another non-pejorative term that fits the individual situation.

As Wikipedia[xiv]: In law, an alien is a person who is not a citizen or national of a given country, though definitions and terminology differ to some degree depending on the continent or region of the world. The term "alien" is synonymous with "foreign national".

The term "alien" is derived from the Latin alienus, meaning stranger, foreign, etym. "belonging (somewhere) else". Similar terms to "alien" in this context include foreigner and lander.

ALIEN CATEGORIES

Different countries around the world use varying terms for aliens. The following are several types of aliens:

A legal alien is a foreign national who is permitted by law to be in the host country. This is a very broad category which includes permanent residents, temporary residents, and visa holders or foreign visitors.

A resident alien is a person who has permission by the government to reside and work in the country.

A nonresident alien is a foreign national who is visiting a country as a tourist (e.g., for pleasure, for studies, on business, to receive medical treatment, to attend a conference or a meeting, as entertainers or sportspeople, and so forth).

An illegal alien is any foreign national inside a country where he or she has no legal right to be. It covers a foreign national who has entered the country through illegal migration. In some countries it also covers an alien who entered the country lawfully but subsequently fallen out of that legal status.

An enemy alien is a foreign national of a country that is at war with the host country.

COMMON LAW JURISDICTIONS

An "alien" in English law denoted any person born outside of the monarch's dominions and who did not owe allegiance to the monarch. Aliens were not allowed to own land and were subject to different taxes to subjects. This idea was passed on in the Commonwealth to other common law jurisdictions.

Australia

In Australia, citizenship is defined in the Australian nationality law. Non-citizens in

Australia are either permanent resident; temporary residents; or illegal residents (technically called "unlawful non-citizens"). Most non-citizens (including those who lack citizenship documents) traveling to Australia must obtain a visa prior to travel. The only exceptions to this rule are holders of New Zealand passports and citizenship, who may apply for a visa on arrival according to the Trans-Tasman Travel Arrangement.

Canada

In Canada, the term "alien" is not used in federal statutes. Instead, the term "foreign national" serves as its equivalent and is found in legal documents. The Immigration and Refugee Protection Act defines "foreign national" as "a person who is not a Canadian citizen or a permanent resident and includes a stateless person."

United Kingdom

Further information: British Nationality Act

In the United Kingdom, the British Nationality Act of 1981 defines an alien as a person who is not a British citizen, a citizen of Ireland, a Commonwealth citizen, or a British protected person. The Aliens Act of 1905, the British Nationality and Status of Aliens Act of 1914 and the Aliens Restriction (Amendment)

Act of 1919 were all products of the turbulence in the early part of the 20th century.

United States

Under the Immigration and Nationality Act (INA) of the United States, "the term 'alien' means any person not a citizen or national of the United States." Every foreign national, including a refugee or an asylum seeker, is considered as an alien unless his or her status has been lawfully upgraded.

A lawful permanent resident (LPR) of the United States is not a foreign national but explicitly referred to as a legal immigrant, especially if he or she was previously admitted as a refugee under 8 U.S.C. § 1157(c). Longtime LPRs can at any time claim to be nationals of the United States (i.e., Americans), which requires a case-by-case analysis and depends mainly on the number of continuous years such LPRs have physically spent in the United States.

The usage of the term "alien" dates to 1798, when it was used in the Alien and Sedition Acts. Although the INA provides no overarching explicit definition of the term "illegal alien", it is mentioned in a number of provisions under title 8. Several provisions even mention the term "unauthorized alien". According to PolitiFact, the term "illegal alien" occurs in federal law, but does so scarcely. PolitiFact opines that, "where the term does appear, it's undefined or part of an introductory title or limited to apply to certain individuals convicted of felonies."

Because the U.S. law says that a corporation is a person, the term alien is not limited to natural humans because what are colloquially called foreign corporations are technically called alien corporations. Because corporations are creations of local state law, a foreign corporation is an out-of-state corporation.

There are a multitude of unique and highly complex U.S. domestic tax laws and regulations affecting the U.S. tax residency of foreign nationals, both nonresident aliens and resident aliens, in addition to income tax and social security tax treaties and Totalization Agreements.

"Alienage," i.e., citizenship status, has been prohibited since 1989 in the city of New York from being considered for employment, under that town's Human Rights legislation.

OTHER JURISDICTIONS

Arab states

In the Arab states of the Persian Gulf (United Arab Emirates, Saudi Arabia, Kuwait, Oman, Bahrain, Qatar, etc.), many non-natives (foreigners) have lived in the region since birth or since independence. However, these Arab states of the Persian Gulf do not easily grant citizenship to the non-natives.

Latvia

On Latvian passports, the mark nepilsoni (alien) refers to non-citizens or former citizens of the Soviet Union (USSR) who do not have voting rights for the parliament of Latvia but have rights and privileges under Latvian law and international bilateral treaties, such as the right to travel without visas to both the European Union and Russia, where latter is not possible for Latvian citizens.

Oh, I'm an alien, I'm a legal alien
I'm an Englishman in New York
Oh, I'm an alien, I'm a legal alien
I'm an Englishman in New York

If "manners maketh man" as someone said
He's the hero of the day
It takes a man to suffer ignorance and smile
Be yourself no matter what they say

Be yourself no matter what they say.

If civilization is to survive, we must cultivate the science of human relationships - the ability of all peoples, of all kinds, to live together, in the same world at peace.
Franklin D. Roosevelt

juanrodulfo.com

SIZE MATTERS

The Office of Management and Budget describes Hispanic or Latino ethnicity as "a person of Cuban, Mexican, Puerto Rican, South or Central American, or other Spanish culture or origin regardless of race."

Hispanic people are the largest minority in the United States. Only Mexico has a larger Hispanic population than the United States.

On one hand White population is declining, and on the other hand Hispanic is slowly growing.

William H. Frey in his online publication: *"US white population declines and Generation 'Z-Plus' is minority white, census shows"*[xv], shared the following facts:

The U.S. Census Bureau's release of race and age statistics for 2017 points to two noteworthy milestones about the nation's increasingly aging white and growing diverse population. First, for the first time since the Census Bureau has released these annual statistics, they show an absolute decline in the nation's white non-Hispanic population—accelerating a phenomenon that was not projected to occur until the next decade.

Second, the new numbers show that for the first time there are more children who are minorities than who are white, at every age from zero to nine. This means we are on the cusp of seeing the first minority white generation, born in 2007 and later, which perhaps we can dub Generation "Z-Plus."

Together these new data suggest that a signature feature of U.S. demographic change in the 21st century is the aging and decline of the white population, along with population growth among young minorities to counterbalance the trend.

US POPULATION STATISTICS

WHITE POPULATION DECLINE

America's white population has been increasing since the first census was taken in 1790. Table 1 shows the change in the non-Hispanic white population using data from the censuses of 1970 to 2010, and annual population estimates for 2011 to 2017, based on the recent release. These new numbers show, for the first time, an absolute decline in the nation's white population of more than 9,000 whites between 2015 and 2016 and more than 31,000 whites between 2016 and 2017. (These new estimates revised earlier census estimates, which showed white gains between 2015 and 2016.)

This is indicative of a general aging of the white population, which means proportionately fewer white women in their childbearing years, and an excess of deaths over births (a natural decrease). The recent downsizing of the white population could reflect post-recession-related fertility declines in the white population, leading to an inflation of white natural decrease to its highest levels of the last six years. The past year also showed a downturn in white immigration.

A NEW "MINORITY WHITE" GENERATION

A second noteworthy finding from the new census estimates is that, for the first time, minorities outnumber whites nationally for each age under ten. While earlier estimates revealed "minority white" status for some of these youthful ages, this is now solidly the case for individuals born in each year since 2007.

Hence, this generation, which might be called Generation Z-Plus, is the first truly minority white generation, at 49.6 percent white, where 26 percent of its members are Hispanics, 13.6 percent African Americans, and nearly 10 percent include Asians and persons of two or more races.

Of course, there is variation in Gen Z-Plus's racial profile across the country. Notably, they are now minority white in fifteen states, including Hawaii, New Mexico, California, Texas, and Nevada, plus the District of Columbia. In each of the latter states, the population under age 10 is less than 35 percent white. At the other extreme, seventeen states—largely in New England, the Midwest, and Mountain West—house Gen Z-Plus populations that are more than two-thirds white. This population is a minority white in forty-three of the largest one hundred metropolitan areas, including Los Angeles, where less than 20 percent of 0-9-year-olds are white.

DECLINES OF WHITE YOUTH

The rise of the minority white Generation Z-Plus has a lot to do with a steady decline in whites among America's youth since 2000. This occurred as more young white people entered adulthood than were born or immigrated to the U.S. However, this trend was countered to some degree by a growing youthful minority population.

Nationally, whites under the age of ten sustained a loss of 1.2 million between 2010 and 2017, according to the new estimates. This loss of youthful whites is pervasive, occurring in forty-three states and eighty-one of the nation's one hundred largest metropolitan areas. This trend has also taken place in over four-fifths of the nation's 3,100 counties. The parts of the country that have not seen white child declines tend to be places that have attracted recent white migrants, including younger segments of the white population. The states of Texas (especially Houston, San Antonio, and Austin),

Washington (Seattle), as well as North and South Dakota are in this category.

Yet these white declines are countered by gains in minorities. Between 2010 and 2017 the under age 10 population showed gains among minorities of nearly one million—lessening the nationwide young child decline to just 276,000. Minorities have not stopped all geographic areas from child population decline but they contributed to gains in the under age 10 populations for seventeen states and the District of Columbia, forty-eight of the one hundred largest metropolitan areas, and over eight hundred counties. Some of these gains are attributable to immigration, but in fact, only 38 percent of total minority growth is due to immigration with the remainder attributable to natural increase. Nonetheless, younger minority populations will be significant contributors to the nation's youth considering the overall aging of the white population.

These new census estimates underscore important demographic mega-trends that will impact the country's future. As older baby boomers retire, there will be an increasing need for younger generations to contribute to a vibrant, productive labor force. Clearly the emerging minority white Generation Z-Plus—small and born since the onset of the Great Recession—will play a key role.

Antonio Flores, Mark Hugo Lopez and Jens Manuel Krogstad, published their analysis titled: *"U.S. Hispanic population reached new high in 2018, but growth has slowed"*[xvi], establishing that:

The U.S. Hispanic population reached a record 59.9 million in 2018, up 1.2 million over the previous year and up from 47.8 million in 2008, according to newly released U.S. Census Bureau population estimates. Over the past decade, however, population growth among Hispanics has slowed as the annual number of births to Hispanic women has declined and immigration has decreased, particularly from Mexico.

Even so, Latinos remain an important part of the nation's overall demographic story. Between 2008 and 2018, the Latino share of the total U.S. population increased from 16% to 18%. Latinos accounted for about half (52%) of all U.S. population growth over this period.

Here are some key facts about how the nation's Latino population has changed over the past decade:

U.S. HISPANIC POPULATION

Population growth among U.S. Hispanics has slowed since the 2000s. From 2005 to 2010, the nation's Hispanic population grew by an average of 3.4% per year, but this rate has declined to 2.0% a year since then. Even so, population growth among Hispanics continues to outpace that of some other groups. The white population saw negligible growth between 2015 and 2018, while the Black population had an annual average growth of less than 1% over the same period. Only Asian Americans have seen faster population growth than Hispanics, with a 2.8% growth rate between 2015 and 2018. (All racial groups are single race, non-Hispanic.)

South region has seen the nation's biggest Latino population growth since 2008.

The South saw the fastest Latino population growth of any U.S. region. The Latino population in the South grew 33% during this period, reaching 22.7 million in 2018, up 5.6 million from 2008. This growth was part of a broader increase in the Latino population in regions across the country since the 1990s. States in the Northeast (25% increase), Midwest (24%) and West (19%) also experienced growth in the number of Latinos from 2008 to 2018.

The states with the fastest Hispanic population growth tend to have relatively small Hispanic populations – and are not in the South.

North Dakota's Hispanic population grew by 135% between 2008 and 2018 – from 12,600 to 29,500, the fastest growth rate of any state. However, the state ranked 49th among the fifty states and the District of Columbia in its overall Hispanic population in 2018. Hispanic populations in South Dakota (75%), the District of Columbia (57%), Montana (55%) and New Hampshire (50%) also experienced rapid growth during this period, though all have relatively small Hispanic populations.

U.S. COUNTIES WITH LARGEST HISPANIC POPULATION, 2018

Los Angeles County had more Hispanics than any other U.S. County, with 4.9 million in 2018. The next largest were Harris County, Texas (2.0 million), and Miami-Dade County, Florida (1.9 million). Overall, eleven counties had more than a million Hispanics in 2018; these include Maricopa County, Arizona; Cook County, Illinois; and Riverside County, California. In 102 U.S. counties, Hispanics made up at least 50% of the population in 2018.

Puerto Rico's population decreased again in 2018, extending trend.

Puerto Rico's population declined nearly 4% in 2018 and has been down about 15% since 2008. The island's population stood at 3.2 million in 2018, down from 3.3 million in 2017, when hurricanes Maria and Irma hit. The two disasters led many Puerto Ricans to leave for the U.S. mainland, especially Florida. Even before the hurricanes, however, the island's population had experienced a steady, long-term population decline due to a long-standing economic recession.

Latinos are among the youngest racial or ethnic groups in the U.S. but saw one of the largest increases in median age over the past decade.

Latinos had a median age of 30 in 2018, up from 27 in 2008. Whites had the highest median age nationally – 44 in 2018 – followed by Asians (37) and Black people (34). The median age for both Latinos and whites has increased by three years since 2008, tying for the largest uptick of any racial or ethnic group.

On their research published on November 9, 2018, Antonio Flores, Mark Hugo Lopez and Jens Krogstad, titled: *"Key takeaways about Latino voters in the 2018 midterm elections"*[xvii], they stated this:

Latinos make up an increasing share of the U.S. electorate. A record twenty-nine million Latinos were eligible to vote in this year's midterm elections, accounting for 12.8% of all eligible voters, a new high. While it is too soon to know how many voted and their turnout rate, Latinos made up an estimated 11% of all voters nationwide on Election Day, nearly matching their share of the U.S. eligible voter population (U.S. citizens ages eighteen and older). Here are key takeaways about Latino voters and the 2018 elections.

LATINOS AND ELECTIONS

MANY MORE LATINOS VOTED FOR DEMOCRATS THAN REPUBLICANS IN 2018 U.S.

In U.S. congressional races nationwide, an estimated 69% of Latinos voted for the Democratic candidate and 29% backed the Republican candidate, a more than two-to-one advantage for Democrats, according to National Election Pool exit poll data. These results largely reflect the party affiliation of Latinos. In a Pew Research Center pre-election survey, 62% of Latinos said they identify with or lean toward the Democratic Party compared with 27% who affiliated with the Republican Party. Among other racial and ethnic groups, a lower share of whites (44%) voted for Democrats in congressional races compared with Black people (90%) and Asians (77%). (Exit polls offer the first look at who voted in an election, a portrait that will be refined over time as more data, such as state voter files, become available.)

ABOUT A QUARTER OF HISPANIC VOTERS CAST A BALLOT IN A MIDTERM FOR THE FIRST TIME IN 2018

About a quarter of Hispanics who cast a ballot in 2018 (27%) said they were voting in a midterm for the first time, compared with 18% of Black voters and 12% of white voters, according to the exit polls. Meanwhile, many new voters this year were young. A majority of voters younger than thirty said they were voting in a midterm for the first time.

HISPANIC WOMEN MORE OFTEN VOTED FOR DEMOCRATS THAN HISPANIC MEN IN 2018

Hispanics had a gender gap in voting preference, with 73% of Hispanic women and 63% of Hispanic men backing the Democratic congressional candidates – a reflection of the election's broad gender differences. In a pre-election Pew Research Center survey of Hispanics, differences by gender extended to views of the country. For example, Hispanic women were significantly more dissatisfied with the way things are going in the country today than Hispanic men.

A gender gap also existed among white voters, with 49% of white women backing the Democratic congressional candidate compared with 39% of white men. By contrast, few gender differences existed among Black voters, with about nine-in-ten Black voters of both genders backing Democratic candidates.

How Hispanics voted in key races for U.S. Senate and governor in 2018

Latinos made up a notable share of eligible voters in several states with competitive races for U.S. Senate and governor, including Texas (30%), Arizona (23%), Florida (20%) and Nevada (19%). In these states, Democrats won the Latino vote, sometimes by a wide margin. In the Texas Senate race, 64% of Latinos voted for Democrat Beto O'Rourke while 35% voted for Republican incumbent Ted Cruz. In the state's race for governor, about half of Hispanics (53%) voted for Democrat Lupe Valdez and 42% backed the Republican, Greg Abbott.

In Florida, Republican candidates often win a larger share of the Hispanic vote than elsewhere, in part due to a large population of Cubans that has tended to vote more Republican than other Hispanic groups. In the Senate race, 54% of Hispanics voted for Democrat Bill Nelson and 45% backed Republican Rick Scott. Latinos voted similarly in the race for governor, with 54% of Hispanics voting for Democrat Andrew Gillum and 44% voting for Republican Ron DeSantis.

Meanwhile, Latinos voted for Democratic candidates by wide margins in Nevada. About 67% of Latinos voted for Democrat Jacky Rosen in the Senate race, compared with 30% who voted for Republican Dean Heller. In the race for governor, Latinos voted in a similar manner.

In Florida, Latino voter registration reached a new high.

In Florida, the number of Hispanic registered voters reached 2.2 million this year, an 8.4% increase over 2016. This is nearly double the increase from the previous midterm election in 2014, when Hispanic voter registration increased 4.6% over 2012.

Counties with some of the largest Puerto Rican populations had some of the fastest growth in registered voters, including Polk, Pasco, Osceola, Lake, Marion, and Volusia – all counties where Hispanic voter registration grew by 15% or more over 2016. (Note: This item has been corrected. See details at end of post.)

Nine U.S. House districts in which Hispanics make up at least 10% of eligible voters changed parties.

These include Florida's 26th and 27th districts, California's 25th District, Arizona's 2nd District, Texas' 7th and 32nd districts, Colorado's 6th District, New York's 11th District and New Jersey's 2nd District. In all these congressional districts, the Democratic candidate won a seat previously held by a Republican.

The number of representatives of Cuban origin representing South Florida districts fell from three to one. (South Florida holds more than half of the nation's Cuban-origin population.) In Florida's 26th District, Democrat Debbie Mucarsel-Powell, an immigrant from Ecuador, defeated incumbent Republican Carlos Curbelo, who is of Cuban origin. In addition, a Cuban no longer represents Florida's 27th District, where longtime Rep. Ileana Ros-Lehtinen did not seek re-election. Democrat Donna Shalala defeated Republican Maria Elvira Salazar, who is of Cuban origin. Meanwhile, Republican Mario Diaz-Balart, who is of Cuban origin, won re-election in Florida's 25th District.

A different language is a different vision of life. **Federico Fellini**

juanrodulfo.com

THE AMERICAN DREAM LANGUAGE

China has hundreds of dialects, but they understand each other because of a common written language, in India most of the people speaks at least three languages, the US Census Bureau published this article: *"Census Bureau Reports at Least 350 Languages Spoken in U.S. Homes"*[xviii] in 2015, and goes like this:

U.S. Census Bureau released a set of new tables today detailing hundreds of languages that U.S. residents speak at home. American Community Survey data on languages spoken at home were previously available for only thirty-nine languages. These tables, based on American Community Survey data collected from 2009 to 2013, expand the languages and language groups tabulated to 350.

These tables are among the most comprehensive data ever released from the Census Bureau on languages spoken less widely in the United States, such as Pennsylvania Dutch, Ukrainian, Turkish, Romanian, Amharic, and many others. Also included are 150 different Native North American languages, collectively spoken by more than 350,000 people, including Yupik, Dakota, Apache, Keres, and Cherokee.

"While most of the U.S. population speaks only English at home or a handful of other languages like Spanish or Vietnamese, the American Community Survey reveals the wide-ranging language diversity of the United States," said Erik Vickstrom, a Census Bureau statistician. "For example, in the New York metro area alone, more than a third of the population speaks a language other than English at home, and close to two hundred different languages are spoken. Knowing the number of languages and how many speak these languages in a particular area provides valuable information to policymakers, planners, and researchers."

The tables provide information on languages and language groups for counties and core-based statistical areas (metropolitan and micropolitan areas) with populations of 100,000 or more and 25,000 or more speakers of languages other than Spanish, as well as for the nation, states, and Puerto Rico regardless of population size. These data show the number of speakers of each language and the number who speak English less than "very well" — a common measure of English proficiency.

In addition to making the tables available for download as a spreadsheet, the Census Bureau will release the data as part of its application programming interface, or API.

Highlights for the fifteen largest metro areas:

New York metro area

- At least 192 languages are spoken at home.
- Thirty-eight percent of the metro area population age 5 and over speak a language other than English at home.
- One of the smaller language groups found there is Bengali, with 105,765 speakers.

Los Angeles metro area

- At least 185 languages are spoken at home.
- Fifty-four percent of the metro area population age 5 and over speak a language other than English at home.
- One of the smaller language groups found there is Indonesian, with 12,750 speakers.

Chicago metro area

- At least 153 languages are spoken at home.
- Twenty-nine percent of the metro area population age 5 and over speak a language other than English at home.
- One of the smaller language groups found there is Serbian, with 17,490 speakers.

Dallas metro area

- At least 156 languages are spoken at home.
- Thirty percent of the metro area population age 5 and over speak a language other than English at home.
- One of the smaller language groups found there is Telugu, with 12,630 speakers.

Philadelphia metro area

- At least 146 languages are spoken at home.

- Fifteen percent of the metro area population age 5 and over speak a language other than English at home.
- One of the smaller language groups found there is Malayalam, with 10,370 speakers.

Houston metro area

- At least 145 languages are spoken at home.
- Thirty-seven percent of the metro area population age 5 and over speak a language other than English at home.
- One of the smaller language groups found there is Tamil, with 4,690 speakers.

Washington metro area

- At least 168 languages are spoken at home.
- Twenty-six percent of the metro area population age 5 and over speak a language other than English at home.

- One of the smaller language groups found there is Amharic, with 43,125 speakers.

Miami metro area

- At least 128 languages are spoken at home.
- Fifty-one percent of the metro area population age 5 and over speak a language other than English at home.
- One of the smaller language groups found there is Romanian, with 5,295 speakers.

Atlanta metro area

- At least 146 languages are spoken at home.
- Seventeen percent of the metro area population age 5 and over speak a language other than English at home.
- One of the smaller language groups found there is Swahili, with 4,195 speakers.

Boston metro area

- At least 138 languages are spoken at home.
- Twenty-three percent of the metro area population age 5 and over speak a language other than English at home.
- One of the smaller language groups found there is Albanian, with 6,800 speakers.

San Francisco metro area

- At least 163 languages are spoken at home.
- Forty percent of the metro area population age 5 and over speak a language other than English at home.
- One of the smaller language groups found there is Panjabi, with 19,985 speakers.

Detroit metro area

- At least 126 languages are spoken at home.

- Twelve percent of the metro area population age 5 and over speak a language other than English at home.
- One of the smaller language groups found there is Syriac, with 23,175 speakers.

Riverside, Calif., metro area

- At least 145 languages are spoken at home.
- Forty percent of the metro area population age 5 and over speak a language other than English at home.
- One of the smaller language groups found there is Dutch, with 2,425 speakers.

Phoenix metro area

- At least 163 languages are spoken at home.
- Twenty-six percent of the metro area population age 5 and over speak a language other than English at home.

- One of the smaller language groups found there is Pima, with 3,050 speakers.

Seattle metro area

- At least 166 languages are spoken at home.
- Twenty-two percent of the metro area population age 5 and over speak a language other than English at home.
- One of the smaller language groups found there is Ukrainian, with 15,850 speakers.

I believe that the US, like China, has been one piece for decades, because of the ***Language of Work***, even though this country is a mixture of spoken and sign languages, races, religions, colors, shapes, I dare to affirm that more than 90% of the immigrant that comes to this country connect with each other and preexisting inhabitants through the language of work of millions of Aliens with over stimulated Brains thriving daily to succeed and push forward the

American Dream.

Peace!

THE AUTHOR

Juan Ramon Rodulfo Moya, **Defined by Nature**: Inhabitant of Planet Earth, Human, Son of Eladio Rodulfo and Briceida Moya, Brother of Gabriela, Gustavo and Katiuska, Father of Gabriel and Sofia; **Defined by society**: Venezuelan Citizen (Limited Human Rights by default), Friend of many, enemy of few, Neighbor, Student/Teacher/Student, Worker/Supervisor/Manager/Leader/Worker, Husband of K/Ex-Husband of K/Husband of Y; **Defined by the U.S. Immigration Office**: Legal Alien; **Classroom studies**: Master's Degree in Human Resource Management, English, Mandarin Chinese; **Real-World Studies**: Human Behavior; **Home Studios**: SEO Webmaster, Graphic Design, Application and Website Development, Internet and Social Media Marketing, Video Production, YouTube Branding, Part 107 Commercial Drone Pilot, Import-Export, Affiliate Marketing, Cooking, Laundry, Home Cleaning; **Work experience**: Public-Private-Entrepreneurial Sectors; **Other definitions:** Bitcoin Evangelist, Defender of Human Rights, Peace and Love.

juanrodulfo.com

PUBLICATIONS:

Books:

- Why Maslow: How to use his theory to stay in Power Forever (EN/SP)
- Asylum Seekers (EN/SP)
- Manual for Gorillas: 9 Rules to be the "Fer-pect" Dictator (EN/SP)
- Why you must Play the Lottery (EN/SP); Para Español Oprima #2: Speaking Spanish in Times of Xenophobia (EN/SP)
- Cause of Death: IGNORANCE | Human Behavior in Times of PANIC (EN/SP)
- Politics explained for Millennials, GENs XYZ and future generations (EN/SP)
- Las cenizas del Ejército Libertador (EN/SP)
- Remain Silent: The only right we have. The legal Aliens (EN/SP)
- Fortune Cookie Coaching 88 Motivational Tips Made of Fortune Cookies, Vol I (EN)
- Vicky Erotic Tales, Vol I (EN)

Blogs:

Noticias de Nueva Esparta, Ubuntu Café, Coffee Secrets, Guaripete Pro, Rodulfox, Red Wasp Drone, Barista Pro, Gorila Travel, Fortune Cookie Coach, All Books, Vicky Toys.

AUDIOVISUAL PRODUCTIONS:

PODCASTS:

Ubuntu Cafe | Vicky Erotic Tales | Fortune Cookie Coach | All Books, available at: juanrodulfo.com/podcasts

MUSIC:

Albums: Margarita | Race to Extinction | Relaxed Panda | Amazonia | Cassiopeia | Caracas | Arcoiris Musical | Close Your Eyes, disponibles en: juanrodulfo.com/music

PHOTOGRAPHY & VIDEO:

On sale at Adobe Stock, iStock, Shutterstock, and Veectezy, available at: juanrodulfo.com/gallery

SOCIAL MEDIA PROFILES:

Twitter / FB / Instagram / TikTok/ VK / LinkedIn / Sina Weibo: @rodulfox
Google Author: https://g.co/kgs/grjtN5
Google Artist: https://g.co/kgs/H7Fiqg
Twitter: https://twitter.com/rodulfox
Facebook: https://facebook.com/rodulfox
LinkedIn: https://www.linkedin.com/in/rodulfox
Instagram: https://www.instagram.com/rodulfox/

VK: https://vk.com/rodulfox
TikTok: https://www.tiktok.com/@rodulfox
Trading View: https://www.tradingview.com/u/rodulfox/

REFERENCES

[i] Human Evolution, WIKIPEDIA, fetch on 8/8/2019 from: https://en.wikipedia.org/wiki/Human_evolution

[ii] Or I should mean those who accumulate plenty of money for nothing and on the backs of We the "others". I do not believe in rich and poor; we are all the same.

[iii] Not Brown Indian jejeje, a degradation of black!

[iv] Ian Schwartz, Bill Maher: The Wall Not Needed Because Bigotry, Racism, Ignorance & Paranoia Is In Heart Of Every Trumpster, fetched on 8/8/2019 from: https://www.realclearpolitics.com/video/2018/02/03/bill_maher_the_wall_not_needed_because_bigotry_racism_ignorance_paranoia_is_in_heart_of_every_trumpster.html

[v] Nothing to do with my brand Rodulfox...!

[vi] Wikipedia, Human Evolution, fetched on 8/8/2019 from: https://en.wikipedia.org/wiki/Human_evolution

[vii] Smithsonian Museum of Natural History, Human Origins Initiative, Broader Social Impacts Committee Co-chairs Dr. Connie Bertka and Dr. Jim Miller, Science, Religion, Evolution and Creationism: Primer, fetched on 8/8/2019 from: http://humanorigins.si.edu/about/broader-social-impacts-committee/science-religion-evolution-and-creationism-primer

[viii] This Gentleman was from Morocco, that day I learned that they use the expression "As-salamu alaykum", Arabic greeting that means "Peace upon you", expression familiar for me because on my beloved Margarita Island at the Caribbean Sea, North of Venezuela, there is a huge Arab Colony.

juanrodulfo.com

[ix] Startupr Hong Kong Limited, October 4, 2018, fetched on 11/7/19 from: https://medium.com/swlh/10-most-important-business-languages-in-global-market-17b49b7cf2d2

[x] Bec Crew, 11/13/2014, How Learning a New Language Changes your Brain – At Any Age, fetched on 11/8/2019 from: https://www.sciencealert.com/here-s-how-learning-a-new-language-changes-your-brain-at-any-age

[xi] Raquel Magalhães, What happens to your brain when you learn a new language? 02/19/2019, Fetched on 11/8/2019 from: https://unbabel.com/blog/brain-language-learning/

[xii] National Archives, What is an A-file?, fetched on 11/8/2019 from: https://www.archives.gov/research/immigration/aliens/a-files-san-francisco.html

[xiii] Elizabeth Rosenman, The Hill, This new year, let's stop using the word 'alien'", 01/02/2019, fetched on 11/8/2019 from: https://thehill.com/opinion/immigration/423570-this-new-year-lets-stop-using-the-word-alien

[xiv] Alien, Wikipedia, fetched on 11/8/2019 from: https://en.wikipedia.org/wiki/Alien_(law)

[xv] William H. Frey, The Avenue, US white population declines and Generation 'Z-Plus' is minority white, census shows, 06/22/2018, fetched on 11/8/2019 from: https://www.brookings.edu/blog/the-avenue/2018/06/21/us-white-population-declines-and-generation-z-plus-is-minority-white-census-shows/?gclid=CjoKCQiAno_uBRC1ARIsAB496IU1HcInofwIm_h4CqigMk_N6g5r7VDobluondaSLur977oQQRx_m5saAhr-EALw_wcB

[xvi] Antonio Flores, Mark Hugo Lopez, Jens Manuel Krogstad, U.S. Hispanic population reached new high in 2018, but growth has slowed, Factank, Pew Research Center, 07/8/2019, fetched on 11/8/2019 from: https://www.pewresearch.org/fact-tank/2019/07/08/u-

s-hispanic-population-reached-new-high-in-2018-but-growth-has-slowed/

[xvii] Antonio Flores, Mark Hugo Lopez, Jens Manuel Krogstad, Key takeaways about Latino voters in the 2018 midterm elections, Factank, Pew Research Center, 11/9/2018, fetched on 11/8/2019 from: https://www.pewresearch.org/fact-tank/2018/11/09/how-latinos-voted-in-2018-midterms/

[xviii] US Census Bureau, Census Bureau Reports at Least 350 Languages Spoken in U.S. Homes, 11/03/2015, fetched on 11/9/2019 from: https://www.census.gov/newsroom/press-releases/2015/cb15-185.html

www.ingramcontent.com/pod-product-compliance
Lightning Source LLC
LaVergne TN
LVHW052245070526
838201LV00113B/350/J